Spanish with Amigos

A Beginner's Guide to Conversational Spanish

Tara Bradley Williams

A Note from the Author

Learning Spanish can be a fun, social activity! I am sure that learning Spanish is something that you have thought about for a long time – whether it be for your job or simply for personal fulfillment. I am also positive that you are not the only one around you who would like to learn Spanish. So find a family member, friend, or co-worker who would also like to learn. Better yet – create a Spanish conversation group! (Or go online to spanish.meetup.com to find one in your area.) Do whatever it takes to make Spanish learning fun – and enjoy the journey!

ISBN: 978-1-934467-72-5

All inquiries should be addressed to:
Pronto Spanish Services, LLC
P.O. Box 92
Lake Mills, WI 53551
www.ProntoSpanish.com

Table of Contents

Introduction

Learning Spanish does *not* have to be a difficult task. It does *not* have to be boring. Learning Spanish can be fun! Not only does *Spanish with Amigos* give you lists of vocabulary words and phrases broken down by topic, it also helps you take your Spanish learning to the next level by giving you ideas on how to *practice* this vocabulary in conversation. Use these ideas as a springboard for more ideas. Get together with friends and be creative on how you can use these words and vocabulary. Do whatever it takes to make Spanish learning fun!

Spanish Alphabet

Let's start out right from the beginning with the alphabet. The letters *ch, ll, ñ* and *rr* are in addition to our English alphabet. Three of these letters, *ch, ll,* and *rr,* are no longer considered "official" letters according to the *Real Academia Española*, but some students still learn them. Only the *ñ* still has its own entry in the modern Spanish dictionary.

The other thing you may notice is that if you have taken Spanish before, you may have learned another word for the letter *w*. There are actually a few different ways that this letter can be said, depending on the region. One of the reasons for this is because the letter *W* (and *K*) are not native to the Spanish language and only show up in foreign words, such as *sitio web* (website), *waterpolo,* and *karate.*

Spanish Alphabet

A	a	*ah*		**N**	ene	*AY-nay*
B	be	*bay*		**Ñ**	eñe	*AY-nyay*
C	ce	*say*		**O**	o	*oh*
CH	che	*chay*		**P**	pe	*pay*
D	de	*day*		**Q**	cu	*koo*
E	e	*ay*		**R**	ere	*AY-ray*
F	efe	*AY-fay*		**RR**	erre	*AY-ray (trilled)*
G	ge	*hay*		**S**	ese	*AY-say*
H	hache	*AH-chay*		**T**	te	*tay*
I	i	*ee*		**U**	u	*oo*
J	jota	*HO-tah*		**V**	ve	*bay*
K	ka	*kah*		**W***	uve doble	*OO-bay DOH-blay*
L	ele	*AY-lay*		**X**	equis	*AY-keys*
LL	elle	*AY-yay*		**Y**	i griega	*ee gree-AY-gah*
M	eme	*AY-may*		**Z**	zeta	*SAY-tah*

*The letter "W" may also be said as doble u, doble v, uve dos, or doble uve, depending on the Spanish-speaking region.

Spanish Conversation Activities - Alphabet

1. Using the Spanish alphabet, spell your:
    a. first and last names
    b. street name
    c. city name
    d. place of employment
    e. items around you

2. Go to YouTube and search for "Spanish alphabet". There are several songs that people have put together that have catchy tunes. (My middle school students especially loved the military-style theme by Barbara MacArthur.) If you're feeling brave, sing along!

Spanish Pronunciation

While there are some sounds that are definitely different in Spanish, overall, Spanish pronunciation is fairly easy. With a little bit of practice and following the same Spanish pronunciation rules, you will be able to pronounce any Spanish word. The Spanish vowels are the key to pronouncing the Spanish language correct. As in English, there are five vowels. Unlike English, these five vowels only make five different vowel sounds.

A	=	pronounced "ah"
E	=	pronounced "ay"
I	=	pronounced "ee"
O	=	pronounced "oh"
U	=	pronounced "oo"

Most of the consonant sounds are the same in Spanish as in English. For example, a "t" and "m" sound the same in Spanish. Below are a few of the exceptions.

C	"s" sound (*after an "e" or "i"*)	**Ñ**	"ny" sound
G	"h" sound (*after an "e" or "i"*)	**QU**	"k" sound
H	silent	**RR**	"r" sound (*trilled*)
J	"h" sound	**V**	"b" sound
LL	"y" sound (*some regions pronounce with a "j" sound*)	**Z**	"s" sound

Spanish Conversation Activities - Pronunciation

1. Say these tongue-twisters aloud. Make sure to help each other with the pronunciations! (Search online for more *"trabalenguas"*.)

   - Como poco coco como, poco coco compro.
     (Translation: Since I eat little coconut, little coconut I buy.)

   - Erre con erre cigarro, erre con erre barril, rápido corren los carros, cargados de azúcar al ferrocarril.
     (Translation: An R with an R cigar, an R with an R barrel, rapidly run the cars loaded with sugar to the railroad.)

   - Tres tristes tigres comían trigo en un trigal.
     (Translation: Three sad tigers ate wheat in a wheat field.)

2. Practice your Spanish pronunciation. Go to Google News in Mexico: https://news.google.com.mx/ Choose any story and work on your Spanish pronunciation for a few lines.

Spanish Pronunciation Tips

- If a word has an accent mark, say that section of the word with more emphasis. (Practice: Mar**í**a, capit**án**, ro**mán**tico)
- If there is no accent mark on a word and it ends in a consonant, say the *last* part of the word with more emphasis. (Practice: espa**ñol**, do**lor**)
- If a word ends in a vowel, say the *second to last* part of the word with more emphasis. (Practice: am**i**go, **ta**co, fi**e**sta)

Greetings

Hello	Hola	*OH-la*
Good morning.	Buenos días.	*BWAY-nose DEE-ahs*
Good afternoon.	Buenas tardes.	*BWAY-nahs TAR-days*
Good evening.	Buenas noches.	*BWAY-nose NO-chays*
What is your name?	¿Cómo se llama? *(formal-strangers, older people, etc.)*	*KO-mo say YAH-mah*
What is your name?	¿Cómo te llamas? *(informal-friends, peers, family, etc.)*	*KO-mo tay YAH-mahs*
My name is...	Me llamo...	*may YAH-moh*
His/her name is...	Se llama...	*say YAH-mah*

Grammar Tip

Note that the literal translations of *me llamo* and *se llama* are "I call myself" and "he/she calls him/herself". However, this does not sound correct in English. Along these lines, as most beginners think in English, they want to add an extra *es* (is) in the sentence to make it *me llamo es*.... This is incorrect. You do not need *es* in this sentence. It is simply, *Me llamo Tara. (I call myself Tara.)*

Spanish Conversation Activities - Greetings

1. Practice asking the question, *¿Cómo te llamas?* (informal) or *¿Cómo se llama?* (formal). Each person will answer *Me llamo* _____.

2. Large Group Practice

   a. First within pairs, one person asks another, *¿Cómo se llama?* and the person responds *Me llamo* _____. When the pairs know the others names, they combine with another pair (so now there are 4 people in a group). Do this until the entire group is together and can be identified by name. (*Ex: Me llamo Bob. Se llama Jim. Se llama Julie. Se llama Carrie.*)

   b. Hot Potato: For more fun and interactivity, everybody forms a circle. One person throws a ball (or squishy stuffed animal) to another, asking his or her name. (*¿Cómo se llama?*) The person who caught the ball says his/her name. (*Me llamo* _____.) That student throws to someone else, asking his or her name and so on.

   c. While still in the circle, start adding the other *saludos* (greetings) before the name exchange. For example, instead of just "*¿Cómo te llamas?*", have students start with "*Hola. ¿Cómo te llamas?*" A few more soft objects to throw may be introduced shortly after to make it more fun and challenging.

More Greetings

How are you?	**¿Cómo está?** *(formal-strangers, older people, etc.)*	*KO-mo ay-STAH*
How are you?	**¿Cómo estás?** *(informal-friends, peers, family, etc.)*	*KO-mo ay-STAHS*
How are you?	**¿Qué tál?** *(also informal)*	*kay tahl*
Very well	Muy bien	*mwee bee-YEN*
Well	Bien	*bee-YEN*
Fine	Más o menos	*mahs o MAY-nose*
OK	Así así	*ah-SEE ah-SEE*
Not well	Mal	*mahl*
Very badly	Muy mal	*mwee mahl*
What's up?	**¿Qué pasa?**	***kay PAH-sah***
All's well.	Todo bien.	*TOH-doe bee-YEN*
Nothing.	Nada.	*NAH-dah*

Spanish Conversation Activities - More Greetings

1. Come up with basic hand gestures for the responses to the questions *¿Cómo estás?* or *¿Qué tál?* For example: *Bien* = Thumbs up. *Muy bien* = Double thumbs up. Practice these gestures with your partner.

2. Have a basic conversation in Spanish.
   a. Greet the person.
   b. Ask his/her name.
   c. Ask how he/she is doing.

3. Large Group Practice: Use the same Hot Potato game as in the previous "Greetings" section. One person throws a ball (or squishy stuffed animal) to another, asking how he or she is doing. *(¿Cómo estás?* or *¿Qué tál?)* The person answers. *(Example: Estoy bien.)* That person then throws to someone else, asking how he or she is doing. When the group has those two phrases down, add the *¿Qué pasa?* greeting to see if everybody can keep the phrases straight.

Conversation Phrases

Where are you from?	¿De dónde es? *(formal-strangers, older people, etc.)*	*day DOAN-day ase*
Where are you from?	¿De dónde eres? *(informal-friends, peers, family, etc.)*	*day DOAN-day AIR-ase*
I'm from (Mexico).	Soy de (Mexico).	*soy day (MEH-hee-ko)*
Nice to meet you.	Mucho gusto.	*MOO-cho GOOSE-toh*
Goodbye.	Adiós.	*ah-dee-OSE*
See you later.	Hasta luego.	*AH-stah loo-WAY-go*
Until I see you again.	Hasta la vista.	*AH-stah la BEE-stah*

Spanish Conversation Activities - Conversation Phrases

1. Practice the conversation phrase, *¿De dónde eres? (or ¿De dónde es?),* as well as "goodbyes".

2. Have a basic conversation in Spanish.
    a. Greet the person
    b. Ask his/her name
    c. Ask how he/she is doing
    d. Ask where he/she is from
    e. Say goodbye

3. Large Group Practice: Make sure everybody in the group knows everybody's name. Somebody starts asking another, *¿De dónde es? (or ¿De dónde eres?).* The person responds, *Soy de ___.* That person asks the next person in the group and adds on to the conversation. Such as, *Me llamo Tara. Soy de Evansville. Se llama Jim. Es de Colorado.* Keep going until everybody's name has been asked and where they are from.

Survival Phrases

How do you say...?	¿Cómo se dice...?	*KO-mo say DEE-say*
What does...mean?	¿Qué significa...?	*kay seeg-nee-FEE-kah*
I don't understand.	No comprendo/ No entiendo.	*no comb-PRAIN-doe/ no ehn-TYANE-doe*
I don't know.	No sé.	*no say*
Do you speak English?	¿Habla(s)* inglés?	*AH-blah(s) een-GLACE*
Do you speak Spanish?	¿Habla(s)* español?	*AH-blah(s) ay-spahn- YOLE*
Do you read English?	¿Lee(s)* inglés?	*LAY-ay(s) een-GLACE*
Do you write English?	¿Escribe(s)* inglés?	*ay-SKREEB-ay(s) een- GLACE*
Yes	Sí	*see*
A little	Un poco	*oon PO-koh*
Very little	Un poquito	*oon po-KEY-toh*
No	No	*No*
Repeat, please.	Repite, por favor.	*ray-PEE-tay por fah- BOAR*
Pardon me	Perdón.	*pair-DOAN*

Grammar Tip

* Add an "s" to the end of a verb to make it informal (*tú*) when speaking to peers, family, and friends.

Spanish Conversation Activities - Survival Words

1. Point to items in the room and ask *¿Cómo se dice...?*. The other person answers if he/she knows the Spanish word. If not, the person will answer *no sé*. (Make sure to look up the word you do not know in an online dictionary, such as www.WordReference.com, if it is necessary for your job.)

2. Find a Spanish word (in an online Spanish article, Spanish-English dictionary, or look ahead in the book.) that you do not know. Ask what the word means by saying *¿Qué significa...?* The other person answers in English if he/she knows the meaning. If not, the person will answer *no sé*.

3. Have a basic conversation in Spanish.
    a. Greet the person.
    b. Ask his/her name.
    c. Ask if he/she speaks English/Spanish.
    d. Ask if he/she reads English/Spanish.
    e. Ask how he/she is doing.
    f. Ask where he/she is from.
    g. Say goodbye.

Numbers 0-10

0	cero	*SAIR-oh*
1	uno	*OON-oh*
2	dos	*dose*
3	tres	*trace*
4	cuatro	*KWAH-troh*
5	cinco	*SEEN-koh*
6	seis	*sase*
7	siete	*see-AY-tay*
8	ocho	*OH-choh*
9	nueve	*NWAY-bay*
10	diez	*dee-ACE*

Spanish Conversation Activities - Numbers 0-10

1. Numbers are all around you. Answer these questions using Spanish numbers.
   a. What is your phone number?
   b. What is your street address?
   c. What is the address of your place of employment?
   d. What is your zip code?
   e. How many people are in your family?
   f. How many people are in the room right now?
   g. How many pets do you have?
   h. What numbers and letters are on your license plate? (A good expression to know here is, *¡Ni idea!* - No idea.)

2. Using the Spanish numbers 0-10, count:
   a. Backwards (*diez* to *cero*)
   b. Even numbers forward
   c. Even numbers backward
   d. Odd numbers forward
   e. Odd numbers backward

3. Large Group Practice: Play *Go Fish!* (Google the directions if you have forgotten how to play this game.) Using the cards 2-9, ask your friends *¿Tiene...?* (Do you have....?) The person will respond with either *Sí, tengo...* or *No, no tengo...* If the person does not have the number you are looking for, tell them to "Go Fish!" - "*¡A Pescar!*"

Numbers 11-1000

11	once	*OWN-say*
12	doce	*DOE-say*
13	trece	*TRAY-say*
14	catorce	*kah-TORE-say*
15	quince	*KEEN-say*
16	dieciséis	*dee-ACE ee sase*
17	diecisiete	*dee-ACE ee see-AY-tay*
18	dieciocho	*dee-ACE ee OH-cho*
19	diecinueve	*dee-ACE ee NWAY-bay*
20	veinte	*BAIN-tay*
30	treinta	*TRAIN-tah*
40	cuarenta	*kwah-RAIN-tah*
50	cincuenta	*seen-KWEHN-tah*
60	sesenta	*say-SANE-tah*
70	setenta	*say-TANE-tah*
80	ochenta	*oh-CHAIN-tah*
90	noventa	*no-BANE-tah*
100	cien/ciento	*see-AIN/see-AIN-toh*
1000	mil	*meel*

Spanish Conversation Activities - Numbers 11-1000

1. To say numbers that do not end in 0, simply add a "y" (meaning "*and*") and the single digit number. Examples: 33 = treinta y tres, 78 = setenta y ocho, 52 = cincuenta y dos. To practice, one person says a 2-digit number in English and the other says what it is in Spanish.

2. Create math problems for one another. One person says the number and the other writes it down and solves the math problem. (+ *más*, - *menos*, = *son*) Example: 12 + 11 = 23 would translate to *doce más once son veinte y tres.*

3. Point to an object in the room and ask your partner about how much it costs. Example: *¿Cuánto cuesta el libro?* (How much does the book cost?) *Cuesta diez dólares.* (It costs $10)

4. Answer these questions in Spanish:
   a. How old do you have to be in order to drive?
   b. How old do you have to be to drink alcohol?
   c. How old are you now?
   d. How old are you going to be when you retire?
   e. Write your 10-digit phone number down. Say the number in pairs (which is very common among Spanish-speakers). Example: 999-222-1234 would be written and said as 99-92-22-12-34.

Colors

What color is...	¿De qué color es...?	*day kay koh-LORE ase*
It is...	Es...	*ase*
red	rojo	*ROW-hoe*
blue	azul	*ah-SOOL*
green	verde	*BARE-day*
yellow	amarillo	*ah-mar-EE-yoh*
white	blanco	*BLAHN-koh*
black	negro	*NAY-grow*
purple	morado	*more-AH-doh*
pink	rosado	*row-SAH-doh*
orange	naranja/anaranjado	*nar-AHN-ha/ah-nar-ahn-HA-doe*
brown	café/pardo/marrón	*kah-FAY/PAR-doe/mar-RONE*

Some ideas to help you remember
verde: Like Mesa Verde (*Green Table*) in Colorado
amarillo: Like Amarillo, TX
café: Like the word for coffee
blanco: Like a blank sheet of paper

Spanish Conversation Activities - Colors

1. Identify the colors of items around you. Ask what color something is with the question, *¿De qué color es* ___? Remember to use the Spanish "the" - *el, la, los,* or *las* - before whatever noun you are trying to describe. You would answer this question with *Es (color name)*.

	Singular	**Plural**
Masculine	el	los
Feminine	la	las

2. In Spanish, the adjective (color) goes after the object and also matches in number and gender. Practice having the noun and the color "match". For example: *el libro verde/los libros verdes* (the green book/the green books); *la mesa blanca/las mesas blancas* (the white table/the white tables). Here are some nouns to get you going:
   a. la casa (the house)
   b. la silla (the chair)
   c. la pluma (the pen)
   d. el edificio (the building)
   e. el plato (the plato)
   f. el cuaderno (the notebook)

3. Look around and say the color of each piece of clothing you see.

Directions

Continue...	**Siga...**	*SEE-gah*
Turn...	**Doble...**	*DOH-blay*
Go...	**Vaya a...**	*BY-yah ah*
It is...	**Está...**	*ay-STAH*
to the right	a la derecha	*ah la dare-AY-chah*
to the left	a la izquierda	*ah la ease-key-AIR-dah*
straight ahead	recto/derecho	*REK-toh/dare-AY-choh*
under/below	debajo de	*day-BAH-hoe day*
over/on top of	encima de	*ain-SEE-mah day*
next to	al lado de	*ahl LAH-doh day*
in front of	delante de	*day-LAHN-tay day*
behind	detrás de	*day-TRAHS day*
close to	cerca de	*SAIR-kah day*
far from	lejos de	*LAY-hoes day*
here	aquí	*ah-KEY*
there	allá/allí	*ah-YAH/ah-YEE*
very close	muy cerca	*mwee SAIR-kah*
very far	muy lejos	*mwee LAY-hohs*

Spanish Conversation Activities - Directions

1. From where you are, give walking directions to the:
    a. bathroom *(el baño)*
    b. kitchen *(la cocina)*
    c. entrance *(la entrada)*
    d. common place of your choosing

2. From where you are, give driving directions to the:
    a. grocery store *(el supermercado)*
    b. gas station *(la gasolinera)*
    c. school *(la escuela)*
    d. park *(el parque)*

3. Take a pen *(la pluma)* and place it on a table *(la mesa)*. Practice giving sentences that describe the pen in relationship to the table. For example: *La pluma está encima de la mesa.* (The pen is over the table.) *La pluma está debajo de la mesa.* (The pen is under the table.)

4. Large Group Activity: Put on some blindfolds and go on a Trust Walk. One person leads another (with a blindfold on), giving directions only in Spanish.

Places

Where is (the)...?	¿Dónde está...?	*DOAN-day ay-STAH*
We are going to (the)...	Vamos al/a la...	*BAH-mose ah...*
bank	el banco	*el BAHN-ko*
library	la biblioteca	*la bee-blee-oh-TAKE-ah*
movie theater	el cine	*el SEE-nay*
post office	el correo	*el core-AY-oh*
school	la escuela	*la ay-SKWAY-lah*
police station	la estación de policía	*la ay-stah-see-OWN day pole-ee-SEE-ah*
factory	la fábrica	*la FAH-bree-ka*
pharmacy	la farmacia	*la farm-AH-see-ah*
gas station	la gasolinera	*la gahs-o-lee-NAIR-ah*
church	la iglesia	*la ee-GLAY-see-ah*
museum	el museo	*el moo-SAY-oh*
office	la oficina	*la oh-fee-SEE-nah*
restaurant	el restaurante	*el ray-star-AHN-tay*
store	la tienda	*la tee-EHN-dah*

Spanish Conversation Activities - Places

1. Incorporate both the Directions and Places in this Activity. Choose a starting location and a "place" where you want to go. Give directions how to get there.

2. Play a word association game. One person says a common brand or name in your area and the others say the Spanish word for this place. For example: One person says, "*St. John's*" and the other responds, "*iglesia*".

3. Large Group Activity: Using all of the Spanish vocabulary that you know (and some *Spanglish*), describe one of these places and have your partner/group guess what it is. If you prefer, play Charades to see if your partner/group can come up with the Spanish word.

Grammar Tip

Note the expression *Vamos al/ la...* on the previous page. *Vamos a...* means *We are going to...* If the word *a* comes into contact with the word *el*, a Spanish contraction is formed to become *al*. Therefore, *a + el = al*.

Examples:
Vamos *al* banco. (Vamos *a + el* banco.)
Vamos a la biblioteca.

Questions

What?	¿Qué?	*kay*
How?	¿Cómo?	*KOH-moh*
How much?	¿Cuánto?	*KWAHN-toh*
When?	¿Cuándo?	*KWAHN-doh*
Which?	¿Cuál?	*kwahl*
Who?	¿Quién?	*key-EN*
Why?	¿Por qué?	*poor KAY*
Where?	¿Dónde?	*DOAN-day*

Spanish Conversation Activities - Questions

1. Brainstorm some questions that you already know with these words. For example, fill in what comes to mind: *¿Cómo...? ¿Dónde...?*

2. Try coming up with a sentence for each question word. See if your partner or group can answer it. (Don't worry. At this point, I expect a lot of *Spanglish*! I am just trying to get you to talk, and at the beginning without a lot of vocabulary, it is hard!)

3. Large Group Activity: As a group, see if you can come up with "tricks" that will help you remember the differences between the question word (For example: How can you remember the difference between *cuándo* and *cuánto*?)

Time

What time is it?	¿Qué hora es?	*kay OAR-ah ase*
It is 1:00.	Es la una.*	*ase la OO-nah*
It is 3:00 PM.	Son las tres (de la tarde).	*sone las trace (day la TAR-day)*
It is 10:06 AM.	Son las diez y seis (de la mañana).	*sone las dee-AYS ee sase (day la mah-NYA-nah)*
It is 8:15 PM.	Son las ocho y cuarto (de la noche).	*sone las OH-choh ee KWAR-toh (day la NO-chay)*
It is 5:30.	Son las cinco y media.	*sone las SEEN-koh ee MAY-dee-ah*

At what time?	¿A qué hora?	*ah kay OAR-ah*
At 4:00.	A las cuarto.	*ah las KWAH-troh*
At 7:30.	A las siete y media.	*ah las see-AY-tay ee MAY-dee-ah*

noon	mediodía	*may-dee-oh-DEE-ah*
midnight	medianoche	*may-dee-ah-NO-chay*

* Note: "Es" is only used in the 1 o'clock hour.

Spanish Conversation Activities - Time

1. Write down a time for your partner and ask him/her, *¿Qué hora es?*

2. Answer these questions
    a. ¿Qué hora es?
    b. ¿A qué hora se levanta *(wake up)*?
    c. ¿A qué hora empieza a trabajar *(begin working)*?
    d. ¿A qué hora...? *(Fill in the blank.)*

3. Large Group Practice: Make a clock out of a paper plate, a pin, and two "hands". One person stands in front of the group and gives several examples for the others to say what time it is.

Months

January	enero	*ay-NAIR-oh*
February	febrero	*fay-BRARE-oh*
March	marzo	*MAR-soh*
April	abril	*ah-BREEL*
May	mayo	*MY-yoh*
June	junio	*HOO-nee-oh*
July	julio	*HOO-lee-oh*
August	agosto	*ah-GO-stoh*
September	septiembre	*saip-tee-AIM-bray*
October	octubre	*oak-TOO-bray*
November	noviembre	*no-bee-AIM-bray*
December	diciembre	*dee-see-AIM-bray*

What is today's date?	**¿Cuál es la fecha de hoy?**	*KWAHL es la FAY-cha day oy*
Today is the (2nd of March) or **Today is (March 2nd).**	**Hoy es el (2 de marzo).**	*oy es el (dose day MAR-so)*

Note that the months of the year are not capitalized in Spanish.

28

Spanish Conversation Activities - Months

1. Say the 12 months in order. You can either say these individually or go back in forth with a partner trying to say them all in order.

2. Ask your partner today's date. *¿Cuál es la fecha de hoy?* Answer: *Hoy es el _(day)_ de __(month)__.*

3. If the question applies, ask your partner the following:
   a. ¿Cúando es su cumpleaños?
      (When is your birthday?)

   b. ¿Cúando es su aniversario?
      (When is your anniversary?)

   c. ¿Cúando es el cumpleaños de su hijo?
      (When is your son's birthday?)

   d. ¿Cúando es...? (Fill in the blank.)

4. Ask the date for various holidays. Either say the English word or look it up on www.WordReference.com. Example: *¿Cuándo es Navidad?* or *¿Cuál es la fecha de Navidad?* Answer: *Navidad es el 25 de diciembre.*

Days of the Week

Monday	lunes	*LOO-nays*
Tuesday	martes	*MAR-tays*
Wednesday	miércoles	*mee-AIR-cole-ays*
Thursday	jueves	*hoo-AY-bays*
Friday	viernes	*bee-AIR-nays*
Saturday	sábado	*SAH-bah-doh*
Sunday	domingo	*doh-MEAN-go*

week	semana	*say-MAH-nah*
weekend	fin de semana	*feen day say-MAH-nah*

When is…	**¿Cuándo es…?**	***KWAHN-doh ase***
Monday, February 8	lunes, el ocho de febrero	*LOO-nays, el OH-choh day fay-BRAY-oh*

Note that the days of the week are not capitalized in Spanish and that the Spanish week starts on a Monday.

Spanish Conversation Activities - Days of the Week

1. Say the seven days of the week in order. You can either say these individually, or go back in forth with a partner trying to say them all in order. (Remember that the Spanish week starts on a Monday.)

2. Ask your partner the name of the day for today, tomorrow, and yesterday.
   a. ¿Qué día es hoy (today)?
   b. ¿Qué día es mañana (tomorrow)?
   c. ¿Qué día fue ayer (was yesterday)?

3. Ask basic questions regarding the week, such as:
   a. ¿Cuál es tu día favorito?
   b. ¿Cuándo trabajas (work)?
   c. ¿Cuándo es el fin de semana (weekend)?

Family

Who is this?	¿Quién es?	*key-AIN ase*
He/she is my...	**Él/ella es mi...**	*ell/AY-yah ase mee*
spouse	esposo/a	*ay-SPOH-soh/sah*
husband	marido	*mah-REE-doh*
wife	mujer	*moo-HARE*
father	padre	*PAH-dray*
mother	madre	*MAH-dray*
brother	hermano	*air-MAH-noh*
sister	hermana	*air-MAH-nah*
son	hijo	*EE-hoe*
daughter	hija	*EE-hah*
grandfather	abuelo	*ah-BWAY-loh*
grandmother	abuela	*ah-BWAY-lah*
grandson	nieto	*nee-AY-toh*
granddaughter	nieta	*nee-AY-tah*
uncle	tío	*TEE-oh*
aunt	tía	*TEE-ah*
nephew	sobrino	*so-BREE-noh*
niece	sobrina	*so-BREE-nah*
cousin	primo/a	*PREE-moh*

Spanish Conversation Activities - Family

1. Describe who is in your family. For example: *Frank es mi padre. Bobbie es mi madre. Carrie es mi hermana. Joe y Adam son mis hermanos.*

2. Now that you know a bit more about your group's families, let's practice our small talk and ask how they are. For example, *¿Cómo está su padre?* (You could answer, *Mi padre está bien.*)

3. Maybe you want to clarify the name of the mother, so you could ask, *¿Cómo se llama su madre?* (You would answer, *Mi madre se llama Roberta.*)

4. **CULTURAL NOTE:** In many Spanish speaking countries, people have two last names - their father's last name and their mother's last name. Women often do not change their names once they get married. For children, the father's last name goes first (in the space where in the traditional U.S. culture, we have our middle name). Therefore, if Juan <u>Lopez</u> (father's last name) Garcia (mother's last name) marries María <u>Castillo</u> (father's last name) Ayala (mother's last name), their child would be named Guadalupe <u>Lopez Castillo</u>.

   Tell your group what your name would be in the traditional Spanish way, with your first name, father's last name, and then mother's maiden name. If you have children, write down what their names would be.

Personal Characteristics

tall/short	alto/bajo	*AHL-toh/ BAH-hoh*
pretty/ugly	bonito/feo	*boh-NEE-toh/FAY-oh*
good-looking	guapo	*GWAH-poh*
young/old	joven/viejo	*HOH-ben/ bee-AY-hoh*
nice	amable/ simpatico	*ah-MAH-blay/ seem-PAH-tee-koh*
mean	antipático	*ahn-tee-PAH-tee-koh*
artistic	artístico	*ar-TEE-stee-koh*
(dis)organized	(des)ordenado	*(day)soar-day-NAH-doh*
quiet	callado	*kie-AH-doh*
caring	cariñoso	*kar-een-YOH-soh*
generous	generoso	*hane-air-OH-soh*
serious	serio	*SAIR-ee-oh*
funny	gracioso	*grah-see-OH-soh*
intelligent	inteligente	*een-tail-ee-HANE-tay*
hard-working	trabajador	*trah-bah-hah-DOOR*
lazy	perezoso	*pare-ay-SOH-soh*
(im)patient	(im)paciente	*(eem)pah-see-AIN-tay*

Spanish Conversation Activities - Personal Characteristics

1. See if you can find opposite pairs in the vocabulary list of personal characteristics. One person says a Spanish word (example: *ordenado*) and another says the opposite meaning (example: *desordenado*).

2. Describe people and things using these new Spanish adjectives. Remember that in Spanish, the noun goes first and the adjective goes second. Also work on the gender and number, meaning that if the noun is feminine, put an "a" at the end of the adjective. If there is more than one object, put an "s" at the end of the adjective. For example:
   a. Carla es alta. (Carla is tall.)
   b. Ellas son altas. (They are tall.)
   c. El libro es grande. (The book is big.)
   d. Los libros son grandes. (The books are big.)
   e. el hombre viejo (the old man)
   f. la mujer vieja (the old woman)

Grammar Tip

For males, keep the adjective with an *o* at the end. For females, replace the *o* and put an *a*.

For example:

Tomás es serio. Laura es graciosa.

Likes and Dislikes

What do you like to do?	¿Qué le gusta hacer?	*kay lay GOO-stah ah-SAIR*
I like (to)…	Me gusta…	*may GOO-stah*
He/she likes (to)…	Le gusta…	*lay GOO-stah*
read	leer	*lay-AIR*
eat/cook	comer/cocinar	*koh-MARE/ koh-see-NAR*
play *(a sport)*/ watch	jugar al/ mirar el	*hoo-GAR ahl / meer-AR el*
basketball/baseball/ soccer/golf/football	baloncesto/ béisbol/ fútbol/golf/ fútbol americano	*bah-lone-SAY-stow/ BAYS-bole/FOOT-bole/goalf/FOOT-bole ah-mare-ee-KAH-noh*
watch TV/ go to the movies	mirar la television/ ir al cine	*meer-AR la tay-lay-bee-see-OWN/ eer ahl SEE-nay*
play piano/guitar	tocar el piano/ la guitarra	*toh-KAR el pee-AH-no/ la gee-TAR-ah*
be with my friends/ my family	estar con mis amigos/ mi familia	*ay-STAR cone mis ah-MEE-gohs/ mee fah-MEE-lee-ah*
exercise	hacer ejercicio	*ah-SAIR ay-hair-SEE-see-oh*
travel	viajar	*bee-ah-HAR*

Spanish Conversation Activities - Likes and Dislikes

1. One person asks the question, *¿Qué le gusta hacer?* The other person answers with all of the things that you like to do, starting with *Me gusta...* Go to an online dictionary, such as www.WordReference.com, to find the words you do not know.

2. Look up foods and activities that you want to ask your partner about and say, *¿Le gusta...?* (Do you like..?) Your partner will answer with *Sí, me gusta....* or *No, no me gusta...*

3. Large Group Activity: One person will start out with something that he/she likes/dislikes. The next person will state what the first person says and then add on his/her like/dislike. Keep adding until everybody has their like/dislike included. If it is a smaller group, go around the group again to make it more complicated. For example:
   - Me gusta cocinar.
   - A Jane le gusta cocinar. Me gusta viajar.
   - A Jane le gusta cocinar. A Bob le gusta viajar. Me gusta golf.
   - A Jane le gusta cocinar. A Bob le gusta viajar. A Michael le gusta golf. Me gusta estar con mi familiar.
   - *Continue to add more people and see how many your group can remember.*

Parts of the Body – Face

English	Spanish	Pronunciation
What hurts?	¿Qué le duele?	*kay lay DWAY-lay*
My ... hurts.	Me duele *(el/la)*	*may DWAY-lay (el/la)*
head	la cabeza	*la kah-BAY-sah*
face	la cara	*la KAR-ah*
chin	la barbilla	*la bar-BEE-yah*
cheeks	las mejillas	*las may-HEE-yahs*
ear (outer)	la oreja	*la oar-AY-hah*
ear (inner)	el oído	*el oh-EE-doh*
eye	el ojo	*el OH-hoh*
eyelashes	las pestañas	*las pay-STAHN-yahs*
eyelid	el párpado	*el PAR-pah-doh*
forehead	la frente	*la FRAIN-tay*
hair	el pelo	*el PAY-loh*
lips	los labios	*los lah-BEE-ohs*
mouth	la boca	*la BOW-kah*
neck	el cuello	*el KWAY-yoh*
nose	la nariz	*la nar-EES*
teeth	los dientes	*los dee-AIN-tays*

Spanish Conversation Activities - Body Parts: Face

1. Start with one person in the group, point to a body part on the face, and say the Spanish name. The next person does the same. Continue to go around in a circle. See how many facial body parts you know as a group.

2. Now that you have practiced your facial body parts, ask everybody you know, *¿Qué le duele (en la cara)?* What hurts (on your face)? If they say *nada* (nothing), move on to the next person. Surely someone has a headache in the group!

3. Write the Spanish names for facial body parts on slips of paper and put them in a paper bag. As you pull each slip of paper from the bag, point to that facial feature.

Parts of the Body – Body

Does your ... hurt?	¿Le duele (el/la)...?	*lay DWAY-lay (el/la)...*
Yes, my .... hurts.	Sí, me duele (el/la)....	*see may DWAY-lay (el/la)...*
No, my ... doesn't hurt.	No, no me duele (el/la)...	*no no may DWAY-lay (el/la)...*
ankle	el tobillo	*el toh-BEE-yoh*
arm	el brazo	*el BRAH-zoh*
back	la espalda	*la ay-SPAHL-dah*
behind	el trasero	*el trah-SAIR-oh*
elbow	el codo	*el KOE-doh*
finger	el dedo	*el DAY-doh*
foot	el pie	*el PEE-ay*
hand	la mano	*la MAH-noh*
knee	la rodilla	*la row-DEE-yah*
leg	la pierna	*la pee-AIR-nah*
shoulder	el hombro	*el OME-broh*
toe	el dedo del pie	*el DAY-doe dale pee-AY*
wrist	la muñeca	*la moo-NYAY-kah*

Spanish Conversation Activities - Body Parts: Body

1. Have one person point to a body part. The others in the group say the Spanish name.

2. Ask your partner if certain body parts hurt by saying, *¿Le duele...?* (Does your ... hurt?). Your partner should respond with *Sí, me duele (el/la)...* or *No, no me duele (el/la)....* If the person answers in English for something not on the list, be sure to look up the Spanish translation in an online dictionary.

3. Now that you know your body parts and facial features, start at the top of the head and identify each one going down to the toes. Then reverse this. Start at the toes and work up to your hair.

4. A fun game to play to feel like a kid again is the game *Simon Says*, or in Spanish, *Simon Dice (*pronounced *see-MOAN DEE-say).* Some useful words include *toque* ("touch" - pronounced *TOH-kay*) and *levante* ("raise" - pronounced lay-VAHN-tay)

   For example, you can say, *Toque el estómogo* ("Touch your stomach") or *Levante la mano* ("Raise your hand"). It's a great way to master your Spanish words for body parts.

Clothing

What are you wearing?	¿Qué lleva puesto?	*kay YAY-bah PWAY-stoh*
I am wearing...	Llevo puesto...	*YAY-boh PWAY-stoh...*
shoes	los zapatos	*los sah-PAH-tohs*
pants	los pantalones	*los pahn-tah-LONE-ays*
dress	el vestido	*el bay-STEE-doh*
skirt	la falda	*la FAHL-dah*
shorts	los pantalones cortos	*los pahn-tah-LONE-ays CORE-tohs*
blouse	la blusa	*la BLUE-sah*
jacket	la chaqueta	*la chah-KAY-tah*
slippers	las zapatillas	*las sah-pah-TEE-yahs*
swimming suit	el traje de baño	*el TRAH-hay day BAH-nyo*
shirt	la camisa	*la kah-MEE-sah*
t-shirt	la camiseta	*la kah-mee-SAY-tah*
sweatshirt	la sudadera	*la soo-dah-DARE-ah*
socks	los calcetines	*los kahl-say-TEE-nays*
sweater	el suéter	*el SWAY-tare*

Spanish Conversation Activities - Clothing

1. Identify all that you and your partner are wearing by first asking the question, *¿Qué lleva puesto?* The person will respond with, *Llevo puesto...*

2. For an added challenge, identify the color (an adjective) that goes with each article of clothing. Remember that the color goes after the clothing item. (For example: *una camisa roja* = a red shirt)

   Note that I changed "la" (the) to "una" (a). Here's a quick chart on how to change "the" to "a" or "some".

	4 Ways To Say "the"	4 Ways To Say "a/some"
Masculine Singular	el	un
Feminine Singular	la	una
Masculine Plural	los	unos
Feminine Plural	las	unas

Clothing Accessories

What do you have?	¿Qué tiene?	*kay tee-AIN-ay*
I have...	Tengo...	*TANG-goh*
Do you have...?	¿Tiene...?	*tee-AIN-ays...*
Yes, I have...	Sí, tengo...	*see TANG-goh...*
No, I don't have...	No, no tengo...	*no no TANG-goh...*
belt	el cinturón	*el seen-tour-OWN*
hat/ baseball hat/ ski cap	el sombrero/ la gorra/ el gorro	*el sohm-BRAY-roh/ la GORE-ah/ el GORE-oh*
umbrella	el paraguas	*el par-AH-gwahs*
glasses	las gafas OR los lentes	*las GAH-fahs los LANE-tays*
purse	el bolso	*el BOWL-soh*
tie	la corbata	*la core-BAH-tah*
gloves	los guantes	*los GWAHN-tays*
bracelet	la pulsera	*la pool-SAIR-ah*
earrings	los aretes OR los pendientes	*los ah-RAY-tays los pane-dee-AIN-tays*
necklace	el collar	*el koh-YAR*
wallet	la cartera	*la kar-TARE-ah*

Spanish Conversation Activities - Clothing Accessories

1. Find out what the other person "has" in their closet by asking, *¿Qué tiene (en su clóset)?* Remember that for an extra challenge, you can put the color at the end of the clothing accessory. Example: *Tengo un cinturón negro.*

2. Ask your partner if they have something in particular. For example: *¿Tiene un cinturón rojo?* (Do you have a red belt?)

3. Find a magazine or ads that are advertising clothing. See how many clothing accessories you can identify.

Pronto Spanish Online Courses

Do you want to hear how these words are pronounced? Would you like more individual practice?

Individuals or groups may also want to supplement this guide with one of our online courses. The online course, *Pronto Spanish Fundamentals* at www.OpenSesame.com, covers very similar vocabulary, yet gives students additional practice with games, pictures, readings, native-speaker pronunciations, cultural tidbits, quick grammar tips, quizzes, access to an instructor and a larger learning community.

Need to learn more Spanish for your job?

When you have mastered the fundamental vocabulary of Spanish, you may want to learn more job-specific Spanish. Currently, Pronto Spanish offers 13 job-specific online Spanish courses at Open Sesame, including *Pronto Spanish for*:

Bank Tellers

Construction

Dentists & Dental Hygienists

Educators

Firefighters

Housekeeping

Manufacturing & Warehousing

the Medical Front Office

Medical Professionals

Police Officers

Restaurants

Social Workers

Supervisor

About the Author

Tara Bradley Williams, co-founder of Pronto Spanish, is the author and instructional designer for all Pronto Spanish books, online courses, and materials. Tara has over 20 years of Spanish and ELL (English Language Learner) teaching experience in K-12 public schools, community college, and corporate training levels and has studied, lived, and traveled extensively in Spain and Latin America. She currently lives and works in Wisconsin with her husband and three children.

Pronto Spanish® has been delivering high quality Spanish courses, curriculum, and online courses since 2002. The goal of Pronto Spanish is on helping adult students learn the Spanish basics and job-specific Spanish vocabulary to help them better communicate in the workplace.

www.ProntoSpanish.com
Twitter: @ProntoSpanish
Facebook: www.facebook.com/ProntoSpanishServices

Made in the USA
Middletown, DE
11 November 2022

14741144R00031